KILLING LIONS
JOURNAL

A Practical Guide *for* Overcoming
the Trials Young Men Face

John Eldredge
& Sam Eldredge

NELSON
BOOKS

An Imprint of Thomas Nelson

Published in Nashville, Tennessee, by Nelson Books, an imprint of Thomas Nelson. Nelson Books and Thomas Nelson are registered trademarks of HarperCollins Christian Publishing, Inc.

The authors are represented by Yates and Yates, LLP, 1100 Town & Country Road, Suite 1300, Orange, California 92868.

Thomas Nelson, Inc., titles may be purchased in bulk for educational, business, fund-raising, or sales promotional use. For information, please e-mail SpecialMarkets@ ThomasNelson.com.

Unless otherwise noted, Scripture quotations are taken from the Holy Bible, New International Version®, NIV®. Copyright © 1973, 1978, 1984, 2011 by Biblica, Inc.™ Used by permission of Zondervan. All rights reserved worldwide. www.zondervan.com

The names and identifying characteristics of some individuals have been changed to protect their privacy.

ISBN: 978-1-4002-0672-8

Printed in China

14 15 16 17 18 RRD 6 5 4 3 2 1

Contents

Introduction

You've just picked up a powerful little journal. This baby could change your life. We're serious. This journal is a companion to the book *Killing Lions: A Guide Through the Trials Young Men Face.* That book is all about process, journey, a season of discovery, and development in a young man's life. So, in the spirit of process we offer you this guide to bring the ideas in the book to the realities of your life. As an old proverb says,

> *I hear and I forget*
> *I see and I remember*
> *I do and I understand*

Men learn by doing. You can read all you want about swinging a baseball bat, but that is nothing like going to the batting cages and taking a few swings yourself. You can watch motorcycle racing all day on your big-screen TV, but it is an entirely different universe when you straddle that bike and fire it up. This workbook is going to take your experience of *Killing Lions* and bring it home.

We've divided each chapter into four categories:

Reflect: First, we'll give you some space and a handful of questions to journal about.

Watch or Read: We'll recommend books and movies we think you'll really love, and that illustrate the ideas even further. A picture is worth a thousand words, as the saying goes.

Do: There's nothing that provides clarity like action, having something to go *do.* This is going to the cages or revving up that bike for each chapter.

Talk About It: Because we're hoping that you will not journey alone, we're providing some questions for conversation with your pals.

Living the Questions

Killing Lions begins with questions; in the first paragraphs of the preface, Sam says,

> In the summer of 2012 I found myself one year out of college and suddenly facing a host of questions. When I left the mountains of Colorado for the beaches of California to pursue a college education, I did it without much forethought. I liked the warmer weather, the campus was beautiful, and I needed to get out from under the guy I had been in my parents' home. Most of my decisions in those years were made impulsively. *Do I like what it has to offer? Okay, I'll do it.*
>
> Then I graduated. After the first few months of elation that freedom and being on your own can bring, I found myself floundering. I had jumped into the deep end of the pool that is life in your twenties, and it felt like I was treading water and getting nowhere. Life was getting more complicated by the week, and my ability to choose the right direction for myself was falling apart.

Before we dive in to the specifics each chapter addresses—money, women, career, etc.—we want to give you some room simply to voice your current questions. It really helps to name things, put words to what you are facing, what you are wrestling with. Sometimes simply naming the questions provides loads of clarity too.

So—what are the issues you are facing these days? Where is life not making sense or getting complicated? What do you wish you had answers to?

CHAPTER ONE

College and Then What?

The opening chapter of *Killing Lions* speaks to the questions surrounding school, work, and finding a life you can love. It is, in part, about chasing your dreams. It is also an attempt to reframe the decade of your twenties, or that period between high school and the thirties.

Reflect

Let's just start with: What struck you most as you read this chapter? What leapt out?

_____

_____

_____

_____

Has anyone offered to help you "reframe" this decade, this period of life between high school and having-a-family-and-a-real-job that is the thirties? What do you feel is expected of you in these years?

_____

_____

My generation is desperate for meaning. And I mean in everything. It's hard to find a category in which some company hasn't sprung up to meet the demand for "a cause" these days. TOMS Shoes gives a pair to a child in need for every pair bought. (I've bought several from them; after about a month they get too stinky to wear in public.) Any self-respecting coffee joint—from the little guys to the corporate giants—knows that people are buying more "fair trade" (no slave labor) products, as do the chocolate makers. Clothing manufacturers have learned that by avoiding sweatshops and advertising their high moral ground, they can pull in customers; I wish more actually did what they claimed. People pay for "conflict-free diamonds"; I have a plastic-free kitchen; even bicycles can be helping those in need through World Bicycle Relief. Throw in ethical eating, which rightfully targets the destructive and inhumane system of factory farms, and I think we have covered every inch of daily life. These are my people.

Do you resonate with that—with the longing for meaning in your life?

And why did God give you such hearts? Isn't that fascinating—why you and all your peers have a heart to change the world? . . . Christianity is all about revolution—*is* a revolution to its core—and that is why God gives young men and women passion to change the world. God gave you that heart in order that you might discover both the joy of being part of his revolution and your own unique place within it.

. . . Frederick Buechner believed that, "The place God calls you to is the place where your deep gladness and the world's deep hunger meet." What could be more hopeful?

React to this idea—does it bring hope? How much of you believes it?

Some of my favorite conversations I've had with friends were late in the evening, when we just started talking about dreams and how nothing could stop us from going to Africa or starting a business or opening up the first newspaper to really tell the truth. Everyone was able to let their dreams run wild those nights. Somehow, under the stars, we felt again that anything was possible. I loved those times. But, like Santiago when he gets ripped off in Tangier, we forget that feeling and doubt creeps back in when the sun rises, and I don't know many people that are moving toward the dreams they voiced those nights.

I feel so bad for my friends. I want each of them to move in the direction of their dreams, before they "change" (meaning surrender) with the voice of comfort or fear. Or they run off chasing everything, anything, hoping something will come of it. . . .

The reason you love *The Alchemist*—as I do—is because the story is speaking deep truth to you. It whispers a promise the heart yearns to hear: *It can be done. Life can work out. Dreams do come true.*

Do you allow yourself to have passions and dreams for your life? Can you name a few?

If you find dreaming difficult, why is that? Does it seem impractical? Futile? Or are things just not that clear yet?

If you could do anything with your life—anything—what would it be?

College is a staging ground. But for what? To think clearly about the college years, ask yourself, are you simply a laborer, a careerist in an endless economic cycle? Or are you a human being, and that heart beating deep within you is telling you of a life of purpose and meaning you were created to live? You see, Sam, the questions of who we *are* and why we are here are far more important questions than how to land a great job and make money. You don't want to fall into a life you end up hating.

What was (or is now) your major in college? Why? Who chose this for you? (If you're not doing the college track, was that your choice or someone else's?)

How are you looking at this time of training in your life—as career grooming, or as the development of you as a person, a man?

Sam talked about this generation being a "hero" generation, wanting a revolution to join. Did that resonate with you?

If you could set one thing right in this messed-up world, what would it be? Why does that issue rile you so?

_____

_____

_____

_____

_____

> If I'm honest with myself I'm a little embarrassed by my generation's way of approaching work—me included. If I've got my history right, in the world before the Industrial Revolution, young men felt no shame to take on an apprenticeship and work their way up until they knew their profession.

Write down your work "history"—meaning, a brief account of all the jobs you've had (for example: ages 12–14, mowing yards for the neighbors; age 19, work study in the learning center at school; 22, just out of school—worked at Starbucks for six months, etc.).

_____

_____

_____

_____

_____

_____

_____

_____

Now look at your history—how do you feel about it?

Can you see a pattern—an attitude about work?

How do you look at work in general?

What are you hoping for by way of work in your twenties?

My generation isn't going to like hearing "you have to wait." Right now, from my phone, I can transfer money from my bank account, while reading the top news headlines, while searching for the definition of a word I don't understand and then translating it into any language (which can then be spoken aloud through the tap of a button), while texting a friend, while taking a video and uploading it to Facebook. All within a few seconds. And you want me to *wait* for something? How many years am I expected to do that?

That is the boy speaking. The boy wants it easy, and the boy wants it now. It will help you a great deal to recognize when the boy is operating—not to be unkind to him, but to choose the path toward manhood.

We raised the issue that there is still a boy in all of us, and the boy often wants to shape our perceptions of the world—for example, the boy doesn't like the idea of this stage being a process, because he doesn't want to wait. Can you resonate? Where do you see the boy in you?

How does the boy in you look at work?

How does he get in the way of you dreaming?

Or of accepting a process?

Whatever else might be going on in his life, every young man is in the process of becoming a man. This is his Great Mission, the deeper stream, the far more important work than career, whether he's joined the Peace Corps or landed a marketing job in New York. You have a few lions to kill before you know you have become a man and that God can entrust you with dreams coming true. Wouldn't it make a difference if you saw these years of simple work as warrior training? . . .

> Exploration and transformation, my son. There is a life you
> can love, but it takes courage, perseverance, and a little cunning to
> get there. It takes a warrior. You are in the thick of exploring who
> you are and what you are and why you are here, what the world is
> about and where God is moving, how and where he is moving *you*.

You are a warrior-in-training. This is the big idea of the chapter; in many
ways it is the point of the whole book. God is far more concerned about
your "exploration and transformation" than he is about the grade you get
on the next quiz or how cool your current job is. React to that idea—have
you looked at your life in this way before?

John talked about the "great battle . . . the battle for your heart, the
battle to find a life worth living, the battle not to *lose* heart as you find a
life worth living." Are you aware of that battle for your heart?

There are basically four types of young men out there:

- Guys who are trying to jump through all the right hoops in hopes of landing the great job.
- Guys who are chasing a dream but are still boys inside and allow things to get messy.
- Guys who are lost and have given up on either finding a great job *or* chasing their dreams.
- The rare few who have accepted the invitation into warrior training—who see this time in their lives as becoming the young men who can handle life and dreams.

Think of the young men you know—where would you put each of them? Where would you put yourself?

_____

_____

_____

_____

_____

Watch or Read

Watching other stories can shed so much light and understanding on our own story. So in each chapter we'll recommend something to watch or read that we believe will be a beacon to you.

We created a series of short videos that fit right along with *Killing Lions* and this workbook. We shot them on an adventure trip in Moab, Utah, and we think you're going to love 'em. Check them out at www.KillingLions.com.

Watch either of these movies (heck—watch both!): *Dead Poets Society, October Sky.*

Which character do you most resonate with?

_____

_____

_____

_____

We talked about one of our favorite books—*The Alchemist* by Paulo Coelho. Read it (or reread it, if you have read it already).

Then jot a few notes down . . .

_____

_____

_____

_____

What about the book resonated with you?

_____

_____

_____

_____

What about Santiago's story can you relate to?

_____

_____

_____

_____

Do you believe you have a "Personal Legend," some destiny to your life God means for you to fulfill?

Any idea what it is? Take a wild guess.

Do

Name a dream you'd love to chase—and then go take a step toward it. (Be realistic for this exercise—don't set your sights so high you can't even begin.) Later in the book Sam talks about taking a sailing class because he wanted to learn to sail. There is nothing so soul-strengthening as going and doing something you've talked about but never taken a step toward. Here are a few examples of what we mean: Take a class—guitar, martial arts, ceramics, or one of the many outdoor classes offered by your local REI-type store. Get your motorcycle license. Join a community theater or improv group.

What would you love to learn how to do?

Talk About It

These journal chapters can be tackled alone or in groups, but at the end of each we wanted to give you a couple of conversation pieces to explicitly engage other men in your life.

What did you love about this chapter—and what did you hate?

_____

_____

_____

_____

_____

Thinking back to those four types of guys mentioned in the journal—which category did you put yourself in?

_____

_____

_____

_____

_____

What are your dreams for your life? Do you feel like they'll ever come true?

_____

_____

_____

_____

_____

Does the idea of reframing this time in your life as warrior training connect with you? Are you willing to go for it?

Field Notes

CHAPTER TWO

Bouncing Checks

Here we dive in to the issues surrounding money—issues that get really pressing when you hit your twenties. How can you chase your dreams when you've got to pay rent? Is Christianity best lived out by the new minimalism? Money makes a lot of men feel like boys inside. And what about God—can we really count on him to take care of us?

Reflect

I've got friends who are chasing the American Dream, friends who are opting for the new minimalist movement, and friends trying to do both at the same time. Really—I think my generation is infuriating and completely disoriented when it comes to money. On the one hand we have watched (like no generation before us) self-made millionaires spring up overnight, and I'm not talking about a million dollars. I'm talking hundreds of millions made from selling an *app*. . . .

But then I started dating a girl who is really conscientious about money and the needs of the world. She'd rather give everything away to the homeless than buy nice things for herself. . . . A friend was at a conference for millennials recently, and the big-name speaker said if we have two T-shirts we have one too many. This is capturing the imagination of a lot of young Christians right now.

Who's right? Is anybody right? They feel like two extremes.

Sam gives two categories of people: the minimalists, who, mostly, deny material wealth of any kind, and their opposite, the "new American Dream" believers who want to be an overnight success and feel that wealth is there for the taking.

Do you fall into one of these categories? Do the people around you? How does each camp make you feel?

The World came up with strip malls, strip mines, and strip clubs. The World is governed by injustice and excess. But making money is not necessarily "of the world." God said, "A generous man will prosper; he who refreshes others will himself be refreshed. . . . A generous man will himself be blessed, for he shares his food with the poor" (Prov. 11:25; 22:9). . . . Money can be the means to great redemption if you have it.

Have you looked at money as a gift from God—as a means to do good in the world?

_____

_____

_____

_____

_____

_____

The World is driven by . . . envy and endless consumption. The World says money equals happiness, so spend your life chasing money. Jesus stepped into the madness like the one sane man in a building on fire, calmly pointing us to the exit when he said,

> . . . Therefore I tell you, do not worry about your life, what you will eat or drink; or about your body, what you will wear. Is not life more important than food, and the body more important than clothes? . . . So do not worry, saying, "What shall we eat?" or "What shall we drink?" or "What shall we wear?" For the pagans run after all these things, and your heavenly Father knows that you need them. But seek first his kingdom and his righteousness, and all these things will be given to you as well. (Matt. 6:25, 31–33)

React to Jesus' words—be honest. Do they sound lofty but unrealistic? Could you base a life on this?

We introduce the concept of "The World" versus "The Kingdom." Is that a new way of looking at things for you?

> So, then the minimalists are right—we shouldn't even be thinking about money or having "stuff."
>
> Well, kind of. When the Scriptures tell us that if you have two coats, give one to the poor, we need to notice the math—you cannot give someone your extra coat unless you first *have* an extra coat. You can't help the poor if you yourself are poor.

The minimalist movement is gaining popularity among many young Christians. Do you feel this is the best way to go? What about John's comment that you cannot help the poor if you are poor?

> Money is like a car—it can take you good places, it can take you bad places, it can open up adventures, and it can do some serious damage. Everything depends on who's driving. . . . Capitalism has proven to be the best system on earth for allowing the working class to better their lives. Look at it this way—the poor vote with their feet. Why do we have to have such strict border control with Mexico? It's not US citizens trying to go south. All over the world, the working man knows his best chance to make a better life for himself is in the United States—that is, unless we destroy our own economy.

Have you felt—or been taught—that capitalism is just greedy? What do your teachers believe? Your peers?

Does the idea that "Money is like a car—it can take you good places, it can take you bad places, it can open up adventures, and it can do some serious damage. Everything depends on who's driving" help you?

But let's take money off the table for a minute and talk about the fruits of our labor. Money is simply the representative of our labor. We are never going to return to a system of barter and exchange—I cobble a repair on your shoes and swap it for the bread you baked this morning. Nowadays we work, in return we are paid, and we use those wages to care for our needs and hopefully for the needs of others. Money is simply the fruit of our labor, and labor is a very good thing and *very* important for men to feel like men. When God created man, it was to "be fruitful" (Gen. 1:28). The first thing Adam got was a job. There is deep satisfaction in a hard day's work. No true man wants to feel like he is a freeloader, living off someone else's labor.

John argues that putting in a good day's work, and feeling the fruits of that labor, gives more meaning and weight to the reward than if it had been handed to us in the first place.

Can you think of a time when you experienced that?

Notice how your heart responds to some of the basic disciplines of money: Stay out of debt. Live within your means. If you don't have enough money to buy that latte every day, don't buy it. It is the *boy* who cannot restrain himself and puts the big-screen TV on a credit card—and then pays twice its worth in interest. You don't want to become someone else's slave, and debt makes you a slave.

How do you handle the money you have? Are you disciplined, impulsive, or clueless?

_____

_____

_____

_____

> Money forces us to grow up; it is a constant dose of reality, and reality is a gift from God. . . . You need to eat. You need clothes to wear. . . .
>
> And that is where fear comes in. I know so many men who make choices based on fear—fear of not having money, so they take the first job they find; fear of not doing well in a field they dreamed of, so they *don't* pursue a job; fear of not finding something better or of not realizing their dreams, so they never leave a job that is killing them. . . .
>
> I received a terrible phone call yesterday afternoon from the mechanic I've been working with to get my VW bug back on the road. He was delivering that old phrase I've heard too many times: "Looks like this is going to be more difficult than we thought." Immediately I thought, *How am I going to pay for this?*

Can you relate? How much is fear driving your thoughts and plans around money?

_____

_____

_____

_____

Money is one of the big places we encounter fear. Fear of not having the money to make ends meet. Fear of losing the money we have. Even in some cases, fear of being handed more money than we think is "biblical." All fear is from hell. Send it back. Invite God to direct and counsel you in the areas fear is ruling your financial life.

> And now the cushion I thought I had in savings wasn't enough to pay for it all, and whoa boy, it felt like the floor was falling out. It was a battle to stay focused on the fact that God will take care of me.

Now we are at the bottom line: what we believe about God. "Either he is our ally, or we are on our own. What you believe about this affects everything else." Do you believe you have God as your ally, or do you pretty much believe that your life is up to you? What do your actions say?

_____

_____

_____

_____

_____

Watch or Read

Make sure you check out the videos we shot in Moab to go along with *Killing Lions* and this workbook at www.KillingLions.com.

Into the Wild—This can be either read or watched depending on your preference, but the effect of the true story should be the same. It's the story of a young man named Christopher McCandless who walked away from civilization, essentially, and his journey to find something real.

The idea of heading out into the wilderness, leaving behind the consumerism of the world, is an inviting and romanticized one. If you are honest with yourself, you might be surprised by the small ways you've left the world behind. It could be mentally or even a posture of your inner world. Spend some time exploring where you have retreated.

The end of the story, particularly the film version, drives home a powerful point—that life is meant to be shared, that we are not meant to walk alone. After rejecting the world it is only on the brink of death that McCandless finally accepts his need for help. This isn't supposed to be the kind of metaphor that slaps you in the face.

What did you do with this ending? Did anything resonate in your need for help in the world of money or finances?

_____

_____

_____

_____

_____

_____

_____

_____

_____

_____

Do

Part of feeling like a man and being in control comes with knowing how to manage your money and take advantage of situations to your favor.

First, do you have a budget? Time to get it out—or make one—and look it over. List all your expenses (rent, car payment, phone bill, groceries, etc.) and then add them up—are you making enough each month to cover your expenses? Do you see any areas you can cut back? (How much are you actually paying for stuff like Starbucks or Taco Bell?)

_____

_____

_____

_____

_____

_____

_____

_____

_____

_____

_____

_____

_____

_____

What emotions arise in you because of the process of doing a budget? Frustration? Fear? Feeling young and inadequate?

_____

_____

_____

_____

Now for the cool part: Name something you've been wanting to buy (keep it realistic—sunglasses, new speakers, etc.). What can you cut out of your monthly spending that would allow you to save up for this new purchase? Buying something you've worked for feels so much better than buying something you can't really afford.

_____

_____

_____

_____

_____

Credit cards have long been feared by millennials because of the damage they saw plastic inflict on the previous generation—but they can work in your favor if you use them well. Do you have a credit card? If so, do you know your interest rate, and how it compares to other cards? Do you keep your balance within the limit of the money you *actually have*?

_____

_____

_____

_____

If you don't have a credit card, consider this: some cards have sign-up bonuses that are enough points to fly to Europe, or Asia, or round-trip to places in the United States. Seriously. Get to know credit cards by doing some online research, and take advantage of the options out there. (Now we don't just want you to go out and get a credit card; this is about growing up. If what you need instead is a financial conference to get your bearings, go do that.)

By being in control of your finances, you'll be surprised at the confidence that rolls over into other areas of your life.

Talk About It

How do you feel about the whole subject of money? When people start talking debt and credit and budgets and savings, do you feel more like a boy or a man?

_____

_____

_____

_____

_____

_____

What are your thoughts about the new minimalist movement? Is this the best way to live as a Christian?

_____

_____

_____

_____

_____

_____

What about John's point that you can't help the poor if you are poor?

_____

_____

_____

_____

_____

One of the big points of the chapter is the idea that "the first thing Adam got was a job," that men are made to be fruitful. What is your attitude toward work?

Have you felt the satisfaction of earning your pay at the end of a day?

The second major point of the chapter has to do with fear and God—do you believe it's pretty much up to you to make a living? How does God really fit in to your deep beliefs about money and security?

Field Notes

CHAPTER THREE

The Book of Love

Oh, the world of women. You can't get through a day without running into the many ways she has been embodied in our culture: music, advertising, literature, you name it. She is there because she has *such* power in her beauty. Move a little closer to a woman, and her mystery comes charging at you like a freight train. Who is this person? What is going on internally? Her mystery and her beauty have the potential to do some serious damage to the young man's soul . . . especially when we give her more power than she should have.

If you have read the corresponding chapter in *Killing Lions* (which you need to do before you try the workbook), you'll notice we divide our conversation about women into two parts. We'll take a first pass here and come back to more on women in chapter five.

Reflect

I didn't have much of an identity on my own; I hadn't for years. I knew that I wanted out, and shortly after my turkey drop I found myself single and happy (well, happy a month or so later).

It was only in that season after the breakup that I began to realize that I had been bouncing from girl to girl since I was twelve. As in, the most time I would spend single or not pursuing anybody was about a month. So, for the first time in six years, I decided not to pursue a girl. I wanted to know what it was like to have an identity outside a coupling. I didn't want to be "Sam and Christina" or "Sam and Liz" anymore; just Sam.

What is your story with girls up to this point? List the girls you have either dated, or took to the dance, or had a crush on since middle school (make a list, a personal history).

_____

_____

_____

_____

What do you notice as you look back over the list? Do you always have a girl in your life—or have you never had the courage to move toward a girl?

_____

_____

_____

_____

Sam admitted that he was attracted to girls who were a little crazy. What kind of girl are you attracted to?

_____

_____

_____

_____

I think most guys down in their hearts wanted to step up and play the part of the hero, the man, but they blew it in their own way by offering too much too soon. These were the guys who knew that their girlfriends longed to be consoled, or pursued, and so—wanting to do what she was hoping for—they told the girl they loved her, or made other romantic promises, and the relationship got too close.

Sam said that "most guys down in their hearts wanted to step up and play the part of the hero." Did this ring true to you? Was there a time when you wanted to step up but failed to do so, perhaps because it was too soon?

_____

_____

_____

_____

First, of course you want to hook up. Nothing on the planet has the power to reduce a man to a bowl of noodles like the presence of a woman he finds attractive. Femininity is powerful medicine. Try and read a book at the beach; it's mighty distracting. This isn't just testosterone and the urge to pass along your seed—that is yet another example of The World fouling something beautiful with one of its scientific "explanations." Feminine allure is soulcraft, my son. Back in the origins of our story, in the midst of a spellbound sleep, woman was drawn from our side and none of us have recovered. We've been looking for the missing goddess all our lives. You must come to terms with this: We are haunted by Eve. *By the design of God*. The guy who pretends he's not has either killed his soul or he has other things he'll want to sort out.

We are haunted by Eve—by the design of God. Does this help you understand your own masculine soul a little better?

_____

_____

_____

_____

_____

We recognize that a number of young men find themselves wrestling with same-sex attraction. And the room we had in _Killing Lions_ to speak to this just wasn't sufficient. But hang in there through this workbook, too, because God has something for you here as well!

If you find you are not drawn to the Beauty, have you asked yourself why—what is that rooted in?

_____

_____

_____

_____

_____

_____

Second, of course it's confusing. You have more in common with an aardvark than you do with the daughters of Eve. Meeting a girl, you might just have well been handed the code of Hammurabi to decipher. This is actually good news—you're not just an idiot, the "clueless dude."

Did you think it was just you—that you were the "clueless dude"? What about women don't you understand?

_____

_____

_____

_____

_____

> Then there is the fear of committing. One of my close friends falls into the group of millennials scarred by the divorce generation so many of my peers had for parents. Our parents—or our parents' friends, or our friends' parents—didn't fight in a jungle or take a beachhead; they fought in courtrooms. Now their children don't want to touch marriage with a ten-foot pole. Why would they? Fear drives them back from relationships, as does years of firsthand heartbreak.

As children of the divorce generation, it is highly unlikely that any of us has been unscathed by the damage of broken vows. Do you feel its power over your relational life—either by aversion to commitment or the need to "do it right"? If not in your story, do you see it in your woman's?

_____

_____

_____

_____

_____

_____

I have a friend named Ash (obviously that's not his real name because if it were we all know he couldn't do anything other than catch things). He went to South America to teach English after he graduated from college. While he was abroad, he met a beautiful young woman from New Zealand who was also teaching. They fell fast for each other, but because she had already committed to starting a graduate program in the fall, they chose not to pursue a relationship, and when their teaching contracts ended, they went their separate ways. Well, when Ash moved home, he crashed in his brother's attic and didn't come out for a couple of months. When I talked to him the other day, he had finally moved out and started working at a farm in the middle of nowhere; he sounded just as miserable as when he stepped off the plane.

Breakups can be devastating. We lose a part of our hearts in the wreckage. While Ash's story might be a "ten" on the scale, have you experienced a breakup; and if so, what did it do to your desire to pursue a woman? How is it affecting your current relationship—or lack of one?

Love is an arena that ups the stakes with each passing year, it seems. As children, we chase our crushes and like them for the color of their eyes. As teenagers, we brood over the girl who seems to offer life and joy. As young men, often our eyes are fixed on the beautiful young woman who keeps us up at night, but we may find ourselves unwilling to step in, lest we blow it. Where do you fall in the journey: crush, fixation, is the girl your promise of life, can't move forward, or moving with strength?

_____

_____

_____

_____

Watch or Read

> Now, by saying she is a mystery, I do *not* mean "forever beyond our understanding." Not at all. Flowers work. Love notes work. There is a *reason*. Guys will read manuals on motorcycle engines and e-trading, but never an article on femininity. Do not be like those fools. Love is going to go a *lot* better if you will learn about the feminine heart.

Right. Read a book that teaches you about the feminine soul. Try *Captivating*, by John and Stasi Eldredge. Lightbulbs are going to start going on all over the place. (Plus, if you tell a girl you've read a book like *Captivating*, it is going to make you shine like a knight in armor compared to the rest of the guys she knows!)

Watch a "chick flick." We're serious. You want to understand what she wants—so watch her movies. *Pride and Prejudice* would be a great start. If you have a girl, watch her favorite. Watch it with her. Just don't rip each other's clothes off afterward. Unless you're married.

Do

This may be a matter of opinion, but I (Sam) once held on to old letters and notes from past girlfriends . . . eventually I realized that they still had power over me. Whatever that particular girl's message was to me, like "I'm not good enough," it lived on by my keeping her old written words. One night I burned everything I had in a little fire with some friends who understood my story. It was freeing, and while it may not be for everyone, I'd at least consider how much power you give to old girlfriends: they will shape your future relationships.

It would be a good idea to sit down somewhere you feel comfortable and won't BS yourself. The woods, the library, the local cigar shop, wherever. Write down the kinds of things you value in a woman; the things you need to see in someone to take her seriously. God put these desires on your heart. If your list is more than "great hips" (and if it's not, then maybe do this with a partner who isn't emotionally challenged like you), it might be clarifying. You want to be clear with yourself what it is that you are looking for and what makes you come alive relationally.

Talk About It

Whether you are dating someone, married, engaged, single, whatever your relational status may be . . . don't go it alone. It is a really good thing to talk about your relationship with the guys you trust. Ask one another how things are going, and have the courage not to fall into one of the two classic poses: the "everything is great," or the "make fun of the girl." Either one probably isn't real.

Share your "love history" with one another, including the kind of girl you find yourself drawn to.

If you are currently pursuing a girl—or want to—pray for one another! Pray it goes well! And if there is a plane crash in your history, invite the guys to pray about that with you too—invite God into it, to restore your heart from the damage incurred.

Field Notes

CHAPTER FOUR

Changing the Scripts We Live By

It's all about identity—the way we see ourselves and how that shapes everything else. Guys, identity is a doozie. Understanding where the root of your drivenness or your passivity comes from can be a daunting search to go on. But it is worth it. This is really, really worth it.

Reflect

Identity is like the turning of the earth—you never really notice that it's carrying you along, but in any given moment you are actually hurling forward at 1,040 miles an hour. This is one powerful force. We cannot live beyond the way we see ourselves. When our world hands us a script, when we find ourselves repeatedly cast into a certain role, it requires almost superhuman strength to defy the gravitational pull of it. Those scripts come upon us from many circles—family, "friends," a coach, a church, our culture.

Is this a new idea—that in many ways you are living out a script handed to you by the influential people in your life? Any idea what that script is?

_____

_____

_____

_____

_____

What were you rewarded for growing up? Was it for being kind, smart, obedient, athletic, etc.?

_____

_____

_____

_____

_____

And what were you shamed for, rejected for, punished for?

_____

_____

_____

_____

Can you see how you are working hard to be what you were (and currently are) rewarded for, and how at the same time you are trying very hard to avoid being what you were shamed for?

_____

_____

_____

So let's think about identity and the heart for a moment. All men, young or old, have within them a famished craving for *validation*. It will not be denied. We will chase validation wherever we can, and we learn pretty quickly what our world rewards, what it shames, what it cares nothing about. So the athletes seek validation by being fast, strong, and winning, while the valedictorians throw themselves into papers, exams, and maintaining their GPAs. The "spiritual leader" latches on to the praise coming from their giftings, and they give their hearts and souls over to that dance, while the "cool" kids go barefoot and wear dreadlocks. We are all looking for the same thing.

Are you aware of your deep desire for validation? Where do you see yourself looking for it—through girls, your work, athletics, etc.?

_____

_____

_____

_____

My friends felt, and rightly so, that God was after how I saw myself. After pushing through the disappointment that God wasn't going to give me a roadmap for the next few years of my life, I asked where this was going. Their question: "Well, how do you see yourself, Sam?" *That's easy,* I thought. "I am a screwup, a black sheep, an outcast. At best I am Jack Kerouac's Dharma Bum—a wanderer who can't fit into the world, looking for answers, being reckless and misunderstood with nowhere in particular to go and nothing in particular to accomplish."

First we must come to terms with how we have been seeing ourselves, the role we have been playing—like "lovable screwup." This can be a painful awakening, admitting how we have been rewarded, what we have been shamed for, and how we have given ourselves over to all that.

Sam confessed the script he was living by. Can you begin to put some words to the way you see yourself? What is the "role" you've been playing?

_____

_____

_____

"Which one do you want to be true, Sam?" my other friend asked. "Do you want to be the Dharma Bum or a king?" It was obvious that I had a decision to make: accept the new identity or stay in shame. I couldn't, and wouldn't, go back to feeling like that. If the lies Shasta had been living with were the same I lived with, and once broken there was a kingdom of our own to be had, the choice was simple. We prayed. I renounced shame and the agreements I had made with "outcast and black sheep."

Sam received some powerful messages growing up and in his college years. Some of those messages were spoken; some were sent simply by the way people treated him. Over time he made deep "agreements" with those messages. He came to believe and accept he was a "lovable screwup," an "outcast," a "black sheep," a "Dharma Bum." Agreements are very powerful things. By agreement we mean those internal choices we make to believe the messages about us. Let us name a few more to help you identify some of the agreements you've been making about yourself:

I'm stupid. I'm worthless.
I'm just a_____ (we didn't say these agreements were pretty).
I'm not a real man.
I can't handle my life.
No one would love me if they saw the real me.
I'm just faking it.

Do any of those put words to your own agreements? Can you name a few more you have made over the years? This can be an eye-opening experience: Ask Jesus to reveal to you the agreements you've been making about yourself:

Lord Jesus, I ask you to reveal to me every agreement I've been making about myself. Shine your light here, God. Bring these agreements up from the depths, out into the light. What are the agreements I've been making about myself?

Pause, listen, and write them down.

_____

_____

_____

_____

_____

_____

_____

_____

_____

_____

_____

_____

_____

Sam talked about how breakthrough only began to come to him once he actually broke the agreements he was making. As in, "I renounce every agreement I have made that I'm an outcast. I renounce every agreement I have made that I'm a black sheep," and so on. You must do the same. Go back over the agreements you've just named and break every single one of them—and the others that will probably come to your mind as you do this!

> We must ask God what he thinks of us. That famished craving for love and validation must be spoken to in a defining way—like he did for you. This is one of the places where Christianity really shines. God steps into the picture to help set us on a firmer foundation than the scripts we've bought into. He tells us to put off the "old man" and put on the new. He calls us his sons. He assures us we are deeply loved and chosen. Let those facts sink in to your heart, and it will set you free. Really—spend a single day holding on to, "I am a son of the living God. I am chosen. I am deeply loved." You will feel things shifting deep inside.
>
> This sounds so simple, but it will revolutionize your life: ask God for validation *as a man*. I cannot overstate how important this is.

This is one of the most profound things a man could ever do—and also a bit daunting. So let's take it a step at a time—start with, *Father, do you love me?* The answer to this one is YES: "For we know, brothers loved by God, that he has chosen you" (1 Thess. 1:4). You are loved and chosen. But it can be so deeply powerful to hear God *tell you himself.* So ask—*Father, do you love me?*

Next, ask God for his validation of you. Now, this is a process, but it begins right here. What do you hope in your heart of hearts God will say about you if you do ask him for words of validation? What do you want to be true of you? Be courageous—admit what you most deeply wish were true about you as a man.

Now—ask God if it *is* true. Pray with us:

Father, I am desperate for validation. I long to be free from the false self. I ask you to speak to me as your son. I ask you to bring word of validation to me. Father—you know what I long to be true about me. You also know what I fear is true about me. Come right here, into this tangled mess, and free me with words of truth. What do you think of me, Father? Am I the man I hope to be?

Pause, and listen. Let God speak. And remember the voice of the Father is *never* condemning: "There is now no condemnation for those who are in Christ Jesus" (Rom. 8:1). If you hear words of contempt, that is the voice of your enemy, not God.

Sometimes it comes in loving words, straight from your heavenly Father. Oftentimes it comes through experiences that at first feel like hassles or fearful challenges but in fact will prove deeply validating if we will accept the lions we need to face.

Earlier this spring I got a call from some neighbors who needed help trailering some horses. Now as you know, despite my childhood dreams, I am not a cowboy; I have only trailered horses a couple of times in my life. But these folks were in a tight spot and needed help, so I jumped in. Turns out they owned some very large, very anxious horses that hadn't been moved by trailer for who knows how long. It was a scary experience. I pushed through the fear, used what little skill I had—and five times that in prayer—and got those horses in my trailer and over to their new stables. A simple act, but it was for me deeply validating—I could handle it.

Name a "hassle" or "challenge" that you had to face but which you came out on top of. Flat tires count. Conflicts with your roommate (or girl) count. Hard exams. Lousy jobs too. If you look at it as validation, how does it make you feel to know you can handle it?

And that is why we must reframe the decade of the twenties in a young man's life. This is the time for courage and process—the season of the Warrior, a time for accepting the journey into masculine initiation. We reframe everything by one simple choice: *I am accepting God's invitation to become a man.* From there we interpret jobs, money, relationships, flat tires, bad dates, even our play time as the context in which the boy is becoming a man. We take an active role, asking our Father to speak to us, speak to our identity, to validate us. We step into our fears and accept "hardship as discipline" (Heb. 12:7). As we do, an inner strength grows within us.

If this were true, how would it change the way you are interpreting your life these days?

Can you make that choice right now? *"I am accepting God's invitation to become a man."*

_____

_____

_____

_____

_____

Watch or Read

Star Wars—any or all three of the original trilogy (episodes IV, V, and VI). Notice that the entire story is Luke's initiation into manhood.

Kingdom of Heaven—this is the story of Balian's invitation to become a good man, one that changes his life and the lives of many forever.

The Secret Life of Walter Mitty—Walter, like so many of us, only dreams of the man he could be. When he decides to *become* that man, his identity changes. (We assume the healing prayer happened off camera.)

Do

Climbing Whitney was a great experience in taking a risk, a risk that ended up validating me in a time when I really needed it. But it was a process to get there. I had to have the courage to step up and attempt the climb; I needed to stick with it hour after hour. Getting to the top (and back down) proved to be a series of trials instead of one simple hurdle to overcome. Maybe it's the process, the recurring demand to overcome again and again, that so many balk at. . . .

This is why almost all initiation rituals handed down for centuries involved physical trials for young men. After finishing their training in a secret valley, the young warriors of Kauai had to swim home—miles in the open ocean. Sioux braves spent nights out on a mountain alone. For centuries the Maasai killed lions. Our elders knew that men learn by doing. It is one thing to be told you possess a genuine strength but another thing altogether to discover for yourself that you do. This is why hard work is so important for young men.

Whatever your background doing physical stuff is, this remains true for every man. Neither of us played sports in high school or college. But we have both found many experiences of validation through physical challenges. This is just deep in the marrow of every man's bones. So here are some ideas:

Look up the highest peak within a hundred miles of you, and make it a goal to climb it within the next couple of months. Invite some guys into your plan. Be realistic for where you live, of course, but choose something that will be a challenge. You'll be surprised by how God will use this to validate you.

Can't climb a mountain for whatever reason? How about . . .

A long-distance bicycle trip?
Joining the local climbing gym and overcoming your fear of heights?
Trying the "Couch potato to 5K" running program and finishing with your first 5K? (Download the app!)
Or how about this one: one hundred push-ups. Seriously. Sam did

this program, and it works—even for guys who never go to the gym. Find out how at www.hundredpushups.com, but be sure to stick with their seven-week program.

Sometimes our greatest fears provide the best opportunities for validation. Do you have a fear of speaking? Look for an opportunity to give a talk in front of some friends—even just a few guys you invite over. Or how about education—did you finish high school? If not, go back and get it done. Is there a book you've wanted to read but were intimidated by it? Now's the time to press through, cover to cover.

All these are about sticking with something to see it through, and you will be amazed at how good you feel for accomplishing that.

Talk About It

Ask one another about your favorite movies, and further still, what your favorite characters are in those movies. Talk about why you would want to be those characters or what it is about them you admire. Your answers will tell you about who you were meant to be. *Really.*

Talk about the "scripts" you have been living by. What are they? Where did they come from?

Do the "breaking agreements" exercise together. Begin by naming your agreements; do some listening prayer for one another to help each other hear from God what agreements each man needs to break. Break each and every one of them—out loud!

Then (and even more fun), do the "listening for validating words from God" together. It is so much easier to hear from God for someone else than it is for yourself. So take each guy, and ask God for him: *Father, what are you saying to David? Are you proud of him? What is true about him as a man?* Somebody act as "scribe" and write down everything that is heard for each man so he can take it with him.

Here's a risky one for guys: Speak validation to one another. Name the qualities you see and admire in one another. (Check out our videos too; they offer some examples of all this at www.KillingLions.com.)

Field Notes

CHAPTER FIVE

Back to Love, Sex, and Women

And so we come back to women. In this chapter we want to focus on two things: understanding the heart of a woman and what makes for a healthy relationship. (This will apply to guys who are in a relationship or single.) Let's start with the differences between men and women.

Reflect

More than anything else, I hate feeling like a fool around a woman. I think most guys do. The sensation afterward is something akin to a personal black hole opening up inside my chest, and I wish it would hurry up and swallow me whole.

. . . I once tried showing off on a diving board by doing a double front-flip but ended up hitting the water face-first and giving myself a bloody nose. Almost every guy I know tells stories of spectacular failed attempts at a date or an introduction or a kiss, and while the stories are told in a circle of laughter, every man's eyes go a little dim as he relives the memory.

Sound familiar? Do you have a failure story when it comes to the world of women?

Sam said that the fear of "feeling like a fool around a woman" is his greatest fear as a man. Can you name how that fear gets in the way of your relationships?

> Now, if the secret fear of men is failure, the secret fear of women is abandonment. This is *so* important to know about a woman's heart. In the core of her being is this voice that whispers to her, *I am not enough. I am too much. If he really knew me, he wouldn't stick around.* Though we all put our best foot forward in dating, we are wearing different shoes, so to speak. Guys do it so they don't look like a fool, and women do it so they won't be rejected. Start with our core fears, and you can learn a lot about the internal world of men and women.

Did you know this about women? Can you see it operating in some of the girls you know? How?

_____

_____

_____

_____

_____

> Stasi is not a man; I cannot relate to her as a man. We don't look at money, or family visits, or sex anywhere near the same way. When I say, "Can you wear a different dress?" I need to remember she probably hears, *He thinks I'm ugly*, when all I was saying is that I like the blue one better. . . .
>
> A woman wants to be chosen; she wants to be wanted, she fears rejection, and above all she fears abandonment. When I make plans

without consulting Stasi, it sends a message that goes something like, *He is completely happy living separate lives; it doesn't really matter if I am a part of this or not.* I may have been simply trying to slay a lion, but she feels it as separation, as a form of rejection. Conquest versus connection. Surely you have begun to experience this.

How might your actions be playing right into her fears of not being chosen, not being a priority?

As you get to know a woman, you want to know her story, the things that have shaped her, because you want to know who she really is. Where did she experience shame, and for what? Where did she experience being prized—and for what? Because everything you say and do is being filtered through her way of seeing the world. . . .

Remember—whoever she is, she has a false self, too, constructed to avoid rejection and win approval.

Thinking of the girl you are in a relationship with—or simply reflecting on a close friend-girl—can you see the ways her false self is operating? Where are the land mines?

And may I say that as you get to know her story, you want to pay *very* close attention to her relationship with her father and how he handled her heart. Their relationship will prove to be something of a Rosetta Stone for just about everything else—her personality, her fears, whether or not she believes you when you pay her a compliment, and what trips her into rage or silence. Does she have dreams for her life, separate from a need to perform? Does she take care of herself? Does she even like herself *as a woman*? What is her capacity to receive love and rest in the security of the relationship?

Okay—we mean it. This is really huge. But first, a warning: you do *not* want to delve in to the deep issues of her relationship with her father and some of the core wounds that have shaped her until you are in a committed relationship. Can you guess why? (The answer is because you do not want to create the appearance of a deep and intimate relationship if you are only casual about her. That is very unkind to her heart!)

But let's go on—what about those questions: "Does she have dreams for her life, separate from a need to perform? Does she take care of herself? Does she even like herself *as a woman*? What is her capacity to receive love and rest in the security of the relationship?" How healthy is the girl you are interested in when it comes to these questions?

All you need to do is look at her friends, the people she surrounds herself with, how she interacts with strangers, where she is comfortable and where she isn't. It is the true litmus test to see if she is healthy. We all create worlds for ourselves that show who we are at a deeper level, much more than our "personalities." Even after one date I could tell that she was different, that she was solid.

Now, there were other girls who seemed a little like

Susie from first glance; they were dynamic and exciting and beautiful. But their self-created worlds, their friends and their effect on others, was more like a whirlpool. They would pull people in and control them through their actions, making everything revolve around them, and when you got to the center, it was suffocating. Those girls are more like drowning women than anything resembling a healthy, independent woman.

Now we are moving into the second part of the chapter—how to create healthy relationships. It begins with some clarity on knowing who the girl really is. Does she have friends, real friends? Does she have a world outside of you?

Are you better because you are together, or are you both stuck in the stagnant water of complacency? That is the first good test for every relationship—especially dating relationships. Is your effect on each other life and a growing maturity and wholeness? Does she move you toward the man you want to be, and is your effect to bring out her best and brightest self?

In what ways is she moving you to become a better man? Or is she pulling you down?

And in what ways are you moving her to become a better woman? Or are you pulling *her* down?

Our generation has grown up with leaps in technology, and as such, texting and online communication are critical pieces of many relationships. I love being able to communicate with Susie throughout the day, but the negative side would be when the couple realizes they don't engage in the real world anymore. A friend of mine experienced this in a long-distance relationship. They would talk online or on the phone regularly, until it hit him that they weren't *actually* living life together—none of his friends knew her, and it wasn't long before it fell apart.

Do the two of you do most of your relating in the real world, or through technology? How do you spend most of your time "together"?

All this gets really messy when things get physical . . . when couples get too physical they really do lose something. I've seen some use it as a stopgap for relational issues that never get solved; in other cases it has eaten away at the trust in the relationship. The question may or may not get asked but it goes something like, "Is this really as intimate as we've been led to believe?" . . .

And I'm not just talking intercourse. . . .

This applies to couples that just make out too.

The church's message to young men these days has really boiled down to: don't have sex. The problem with this (or one of the problems) is that it ignores the core issues of the internal world. Be honest—how physical has the relationship gotten, and is it healthy for her heart? For yours? Do you spend more time making out than you do doing stuff together like biking, running, going to movies or museums? What are you actually *doing* to cultivate a healthy relationship?

Taking care of her heart and taking care of yours will also give guys a whole new framework for thinking about masturbation and porn. It's not just, "Hey—stop it." They are issues of the *heart*. I don't want to give my heart there because I want my heart free and whole, and because I want to be totally present as a friend and a lover. When I turn to masturbation, I'm turning away from relationship. When I lust over a woman's body, I am in that moment turning away from *my* woman. I want the real deal—the wild and precious gift of being in love and offering a strong love, a man's love to a woman.

That really shows the difference between love and infatuation: when you are thinking more for her benefit and loving out of a desire to see her thrive . . . when it is selfless *and* the relationship can stand without the physical, then I think you are on to something more.

How would you rate yourself? Can your relationship stand without the physical?

That girl has a right to know where you are headed, cowboy, before she just up and rides off with you. Mom and I shared in the adventure of the theater company we were starting; we knew this was the city we wanted to be living in; we loved the church we were committed to; and we had a healthy community around us. I don't think a young man should marry hoping that once he does, everything else will just sort of fall into place.

What is the adventure you are inviting the woman to join? Can you put some words to what you want it to be?

BACK TO LOVE, SEX, AND WOMEN

Watch or Read

Bella—this one blew me (Sam) out of the water. Partly because of the sorrow that José is living with, partly because of how he chooses to rise out of his past for the sake of a woman.

How is José's woundedness shaping the way he is living his life?

How does he fight for Nina's heart?

Do

First—did you read *Captivating* or another book on the feminine soul? If not, now's the time to read it.

If you want to take a step toward a girl, what step can you take? Ask her to coffee? Even better, is there a group thing going on at church or with friends you can invite her to? And . . . when will you do it? What is your *plan*?

If you are in a relationship, what step can you take to get out of the routine and move toward an even healthier relationship? And . . . when will you do it? What is your *plan*?

_____

_____

_____

_____

If you don't know the story of the woman you are beginning to get serious with, ask her to tell you. Where did she grow up? What was elementary school like? Who were her close friends growing up? What did she love to do as a girl? How was high school for her? What are her dreams for her life?

Talk About It

A word of advice: before unloading all the difficult aspects of your relationship onto your guy friends or mentors or even your family, remember that they don't experience your relationship in the day-to-day moments; and if all you ever tell them is negative, that's all they will ever see. Talk about the positive too. It's important to talk about the challenges, but it's also important to be the advocate of your relationship.

That being said, ask one another how things are going in the relationship.

What are you looking for in a relationship?

_____

_____

_____

_____

What are you doing to cultivate that? What adventures have you been able to go on, as a couple?

_____

_____

_____

_____

_____

Ask each other if you know your significant other's story and what makes her her.

_____

_____

_____

_____

_____

    If there are some sexual struggles going on, your small group of guys is the place to talk about it. Let your brothers in. Ask them to pray with you and for you. The prayer for sexual wholeness we provided at the back of the book—pray it! It is really, really helpful.

Field Notes

CHAPTER SIX

Decisions, Decisions

The twenties sure feel like the decade of decision making, don't they? It starts with, "What do I do after high school? College? Work? Stay home? Move out?" And the decisions feel like they just get weightier sand weightier: "What do I do *after* college? Should I pursue this girl? Do I chase a dream or focus on my work?"

We want to try and lift the pressure off, while giving you some really simple tools to help clear the air and bring clarity.

Reflect

Start with your immediate questions—what are you trying to figure out these days? What decisions do you have to make?

_____

_____

_____

_____

_____

_____

And how are you going about that right now? (This will shed some light on how you operate.) Are you avoiding making decisions? Stalling? Going with your hunches? Trying to please someone? Be honest.

_____

_____

_____

_____

_____

> A limitless universe of options is not a gift, not even an opportunity to dream; it is overwhelming. Paralyzing. And untrue. You can't do everything. The future is not an endless horizon before you; you cannot simply head off in any direction. Given who you are and how you're wired, Sam, you will never, ever be a professional baseball player, concert cellist, orthopedic surgeon, mathematician, or member of parliament. You get my point. The list is actually quite long. When you consider your age, your situation, your gifting and training, the country in which you live, the economic forecast, I think you'll find that the horizon is not nearly as vast as you have been told—or as the Internet makes it seem.

Have you felt that "paralyzing" as you think about your future?

_____

_____

_____

_____

> The truth is, the options before you are limited _and that is a great relief._ The open ocean is beautiful to look at, but terrifying if you have to navigate it in a small boat. But you are not facing the open ocean.

Does it feel like a relief?

_____

_____

_____

_____

Let's go ahead and get immensely practical (this is a workbook, after all). Make a list here of the big decisions you are facing or will face in the next year or so.

_____

_____

_____

_____

_____

_____

_____

_____

_____

> Remember, we are reframing a decade. Exploration and transformation. As Kierkegaard said with such kindness, "Do not fly so high with your decisions that you forget that a decision is but a beginning." Your decisions are meaningful, but not irrevocable, especially in your twenties.

How does the whole concept of "reframing a decade" change the way you look at these decisions? If you knew that you did not have to make the one right choice that will set you on a path for the rest of your life, but rather see yourself as God's son who he is training, and this time in life is mostly about exploration and transformation—how does that shift your perspective?

_____

_____

_____

_____

_____

_____

_____

_____

_____

_____

_____

_____

Take a deep breath. Let's talk about the *pro*cess of decision making. You are choosing the road less traveled by choosing to leave adolescence behind. You are countercultural already! Maturity grows as we accept the constraints that are before us—the boy will never be an astronaut. You will never work in medicine. Even more importantly, let us remember we are sons. God really does have a path for us if we will seek it with all our hearts. So let me offer a few questions/categories I have found immensely helpful when I'm trying to get clarity.

Choose one or two decisions you need to make, and let's apply these questions to them:

Am I doing something impulsive? The boy never wants to wait, and he can get us into some real trouble. Are you impulsive?

_____

_____

_____

_____

_____

_____

Is t*his wise?* How many people have you asked for counsel? It takes humility to ask advice. Young men are renowned for wanting to make decisions on their own, but that is the first sign of a lack of wisdom. What does wisdom say about the decision you are facing?

_____

_____

_____

_____

_____

_____

What do my friends, family, mentors think? Guys come under a lot of false pressure trying to figure life out on our own. Breathe the fresh air of knowing you were never meant to make weighty decisions on your own. Not even Jesus tried to figure life out on his own. So—whose opinion have you asked, and what do they say?

_____

_____

_____

_____

How much of my false self / woundedness is actually fueling this decision (or indecision)? What are you prone to do when it comes to making decisions? Are you typically driven by a desire to please others? Are you ruled by insecurity? Can you name how your brokenness might affect your decision?

_____

_____

_____

Am I holding back from stepping up? As a man, this is something I always need to watch out for. Given our core fear of failure—read, *being the fool*—and given the DNA we got from Adam, who was paralyzed in his moment of greatest trial, I need to be honest with myself and ask, *Is it simply fear that has me "confused" right now?* Confusion is a nice way out of tough decisions. . . . Paralysis (masquerading as "confusion") haunts every man when a looming decision will require a lot of us. God is here to help us with our fears, but only once we name it as fear and not hide behind, "I just don't know what to do."

_____

_____

_____

So—are you holding back from stepping up? What would stepping up look like here?

_____

_____

_____

What do I sense God saying about this? You are friends with the brightest person in the universe—have you asked his opinion on the matter? How are you seeking God's counsel?

Watch or Read

180° South is a good example of the many "young man looking for meaning" adventure films so popular these days. This documentary would be worth your time.

How does Jeff go about his decision making?

Bring the categories we've talked about to his story: Where is he impulsive? Unwise? Who does he seek counsel from? Where does he need to "step up and play the man"? Can you see his false self playing into the way he approaches his life? Does he seek God?

_____

_____

_____

_____

Read Dallas Willard's book *Hearing God* or *Walking with God* (Eldredge).

Do

> Now, learning to hear the voice of God, learning to recognize his counsel, is something we grow into. But my goodness—take the time to cultivate this in your life. Over the course of his journey, Santiago gets better and better at reading the signs, or "omens." . . . Yes, it can be frustrating at times, waiting for his guidance—don't let the boy sabotage this with his impatience. . . .
>
> God speaks in all sorts of creative and playful ways. The real issue is, are we willing to listen?

Learning to hear God's voice might be the single most valuable thing for your life—and therefore, may be *the* key to "exploration and transformation." So—spend some time learning how to listen. Find an environment where you can be completely still and free from the hum of civilization (typically, this is going to be out in nature somewhere). You don't need to hike the Continental Divide to find quiet, but you should find a quiet place away from your normal routine.

Take a day of solitude there. We call them "solos," because you may feel very alone for the first time in a while. You'll get stupid top 40 songs stuck in your head, replay old conversations, and generally distract yourself with every snap of a twig . . . but stick with it. Ask God to speak to you. Ask him what he thinks of you, what he has for you. Ask him to speak to those places where you have doubt and need to make a choice.

Solos are tough challenges for anyone, but they are some of the most rewarding experiences if you take them seriously and get somewhere remote, turn off your cell phone, pack some food, and head into the quiet for a day.

You'll be amazed at what you hear in those quiet moments.

Talk About It

This might be an opportunity to talk not to peers but to someone you respect and trust. A professor, an uncle, your father, the old mechanic you've worked for, whoever it is, take hia advice with a grain of salt and ask God to interpret it for you . . . but ask him for counsel. Take your questions to the men you respect in your life and ask them. Crazy thought, huh?

Have your guys watch *180° South* with you and then talk about it together.

How does Jeff go about his decision making? Where is he impulsive? Unwise?

Who does he seek counsel from? Where does he need to "step up and play the man"?

_____
_____
_____
_____
_____
_____
_____
_____
_____
_____

Can you see his false self playing into the way he approaches his life? Does he seek God?

_____
_____
_____
_____
_____
_____
_____
_____
_____
_____

Field Notes

CHAPTER SEVEN

Fighting for Your Life

Men, this might be the most critical chapter of all because it holds the keys to so many other realms of your life—your relationships, your dreams, your decision making. Even money issues. You were born into a savage war. This must become central to how you interpret your life because the enemy doesn't stop assaulting simply because you choose to ignore him. It might be a good idea to pray before jumping in:

Jesus, I take my place in you right now. I ask your love and your life to fill me and surround me. Open my eyes, Lord, to the battle raging against me. Give me eyes to see what is really going on here. I ask your Spirit to bring me to the truth of this chapter on warfare. Strengthen the warrior in me. In Jesus' name, amen.

Reflect

We open the chapter with the story of Sam in Malaysia, and his friend Trevor passing out on the bathroom floor. Then John raises a major flag . . .

Trevor's cry also reveals something striking, something glaringly absent from his view of the world. I really don't think I'm making too much of it when I say that it reveals what most people believe—that God is the only other player in our stories. "Why God?" meaning, *Why did you do this*, or at best, *Why didn't you intervene?*

Sound familiar? Do you have some stories of particularly tough days, weeks, or years that you have been interpreting as "just life"? Be honest—when your life breaks down, who do you typically blame? Yourself, God, others . . . or the enemy?

My son, listen very carefully now because what I am about to say might be the single most important thing I give you for navigating these coming years:

You were born into a savage war.

All the pain and injustice you described—these are not thousands of random tragedies, millions of isolated occurrences of disappointment or even human corruption. These are the outbreaks of an epic battle. You must understand where this is coming from: there are dark and powerful forces set upon the destruction of the human race. Evil is real. Satan is real. Honestly—I don't know how much more evidence it is going to take to wake a sleeping world.

What do you think? Can you accept it? Why—or why not?

> I gotta say that during my four years at a Christian college,
> I rarely heard anything like this. "Spirituality" kind of fell
> into one of two categories: either it was something that the
> charismatics were into or it was blown off completely. I
> don't mean being spiritual; I mean dealing with a "spiritual
> realm." Quite frankly, what I remember are a few speak-
> ers and professors leaning heavily on the verses that point
> to something like, "Jesus fights for you, leave it to him."
>
>   I think we don't engage in this sort of spirituality
> because we don't really believe it to be true. We have been
> taught about and generally understand things like UV rays
> and the current value of the dollar, which we can't see, but
> is . . . scientific; whereas the people who do believe that
> demons are real, to the point of talking about them or pray-
> ing against them, look like nut jobs, frankly. Spiritual warfare
> sounds like some sort of Christian conspiracy theory.

Which category do the people in your life fall into—ignoring warfare,
accepting it but never really dealing with it, or relegating it to more
"charismatic" people? Where do your parents fall? Your friends? Your church?

As we try to make clear in the book, warfare was absolutely central to Jesus' worldview. He directly dealt with it when he needed to and then moved on, as did his disciples, as did Paul:

> In the synagogue there was a man possessed by a demon, an evil spirit. He cried out at the top of his voice, "Ha! What do you want with us, Jesus of Nazareth? Have you come to destroy us? I know who you are—the Holy One of God!"
>
> "Be quiet!" Jesus said sternly. "Come out of him!" (Luke 4:33–35)
>
> Jesus was driving out a demon that was mute. When the demon left, the man who had been mute spoke, and the crowd was amazed. (Luke 11:14)
>
> If I drive out demons by the Spirit of God, then the kingdom of God has come upon you. (Matt. 12:28)
>
> The seventy-two returned with joy and said, "Lord, even the demons submit to us in your name." (Luke 10:17)
>
> Once when we were going to the place of prayer, we were met by a slave girl who had a spirit by which she predicted the future. She earned a great deal of money for her owners by fortune-telling. This girl followed Paul and the rest of us, shouting, "These men are servants of the Most High God, who are telling you the way to be saved." She kept this up for many days. Finally Paul became so troubled that he turned around and said to the spirit, "In the name of Jesus Christ I command you to come out of her!" At that moment the spirit left her. (Acts 16:16–18)

So—what do you do with the biblical evidence? Does it strengthen your resolve to take your stand against your enemy, or are you trying to dodge it because it makes you uncomfortable?

_____

_____

_____

Why did God make you and every single man who came before you a warrior? It is a fascinating question and one that deserves a thoughtful answer. Why do little boys understand without even being told that they must take up arms? . . . Why are the favorite video games of young men games of battle, war, epic conflict? The warrior is so deep in the soul of man you cannot understand yourself as a man without it. . . .

Time for a confession: I love *Halo*, always have, and probably always will in some respect. . . .

If you told me that this life we are living, the reality that surrounds us, was so epic, so urgent, so mythic, I don't know what could make me happier. There was something to the story that struck a chord in so many of us. We want to be needed, powerful, and central even.

Name your favorite movies, stories, and video games. What role does evil play in them? What does the hero have to do?

_____

_____

_____

_____

If there isn't a great battle to fight, what are you supposed to do with the warrior heart God put in you?

_____

_____

_____

_____

> All you need to do is look at the devastation of the world and you get some inkling of just how vast, brutal, and urgent this battle really is.
>
> Your dreams are opposed; your love is opposed; your life is opposed. Finding your place is opposed; breaking through the barriers is opposed; things as simple as a date and momentous as a friendship are opposed. Let the warrior arise! Learn to fight this stuff, not only for yourself but on behalf of others.

Just let it all be true for a moment—what would the reality of the battle do to your interpretation of events, of your life?

_____

_____

_____

_____

> This morning I was jumped by discouragement. This is going to sound pretty wimpy, but my truck wouldn't start and it almost took me out, because I worked on it for two weeks, finally having to replace the alternator (for $750). I thought I was done being stranded in various places, but this morning I heard that powerless *click-click-click* when I went to start it up. What came next wasn't merely my frustration; the enemy was crouching nearby, like a lion in the grass, waiting to pounce. Discouragement came on so

thick and heavy, my heart was sinking before I could even rouse a response. Had I waited for my feelings to change, it might have lasted days, and taken down a lot else with it. "I reject this discouragement, in the name of Jesus." That was the first step—do not give way to it. NO!

This might be the most common kind of warfare you'll need to fight—rejecting the lies and "breaking agreements" with the messages of the enemy. We say, "*No!* No, I am not giving way to this. No, I am not surrendering my heart to that. *No.*" Our enemy is a brilliant liar who bases his attacks on ancient cunning and personal knowledge of what deceptions will work with us.

So—what agreements have you been making with your enemy? Can you name them? (You took a pass at this back in the chapter on identity—maybe go back and grab those too. Write them down again here.) Here are a few more to help you name yours:

> *I suck at life.*
> *I'll never be a man.*
> *Nobody really loves me.*
> *Why bother? It's just not worth it.*
> *I'm on my own—everything is up to me.*

_____

_____

_____

_____

_____

_____

_____

_____

_____

_____

_____

Another way of identifying agreements is: What do you say to yourself when things go wrong? Or when you screw something up? What comes out of you? (Is it things like, "I'm such an idiot," or, "This is what always happens to me," or, "I'm such a _____"?) Or, sometimes we make an "agreement" with feelings like shame, or fear, or doubt. Can you name the historic battles of your life—what you wrestle with on a pretty regular basis?

_____

_____

_____

_____

Now—break those agreements! It goes like this:

In the name of Jesus I renounce every agreement I have been making with [What is it? Name it—either the fear, doubt, shame stuff, or the specific sentences like "Nobody likes me; I suck at this; I'm just not a man."]. *I reject this in the name of Jesus, and I reject every claim I have given it in my life. I invite Jesus right here, to come and take the place of this.*

This next step is where we find ourselves facing something stubborn—like when you wake up to fear in the night after a scary dream, or you find yourself battling with sexual temptation for the thousandth time.

"I bring the cross of Jesus Christ against this," is how I continued. "I reject discouragement and I bring the cross of Jesus Christ against it. I banish this in the name of Jesus." Simple, even mundane, but this is where it happens, in the day-to-day battles, the garden-variety attacks like accusation or shame or fear. At least, this is where we learn to fight it, before the big boys come crashing in.

What battle of yours can you begin to practice this in? (Don't pick the mother of all battles to start with; that's like jumping in the ring with Mike Tyson when you have never boxed before.) But do pick something real, and take it on like you mean it—no half-hearted swing here:

> In the name of Jesus Christ I renounce this attack. I bring the cross of Jesus Christ against *[What is it? Fear? Lust? Everything always breaking on you?]*. I renounce this evil, and I cut it off from me by the cross and blood of Jesus Christ. I renounce every claim I have given it, and I banish this from my life, in Jesus' name.

Practice this for a week or two, and you are going to love: 1) the freedom and relief that comes, and 2) the sense that a warrior really is rising in you!

Watch or Read

Pick any one of your favorite movies and watch it with this framework in mind—that it is telling you of the great battle you are living in. (Or if we may suggest a few, watch any of the *Lord of the Rings* or *Hobbit movies*.) Do you see it with new eyes?

Listen to this talk on warfare training—*A Battle to Fight,* which you

can find on the Ransomed Heart website: http://store.ransomedheart
.com/a-battle-to-fight-spiritual-warfare-for-men-2nd-edition.html.

Read a book on spiritual warfare. Try Neil Anderson's *Victory over the Darkness* or *Spiritual Warfare* by Timothy Warner. They will equip you to be a far more effective warrior. Or read *Wild at Heart* (John's classic book on men becoming warriors).

Do

We included a few prayers at the end of the book to help you hone your skills. "The Daily Prayer" will surprise you with the level of fog it lifts and the amount of breakthrough it will usher in. Pray it every day for a week. Notice how much better you feel.

Something else as well: pray out loud. This can feel really wacky at first for some people, so do it in a private place, but really try to find a way to pray aloud. There is a shift in our posture when we move from praying in our heads to out loud, some inner choice that can bring passion to our words.

Talk About It

Share your reactions to this chapter with your guys—what do you think about all this, really?

Now describe for your friends a very real battle in your life. Talk about the role of warfare in it. Pray together to break the attack! (There is so much power in praying together. As Jesus said in Matthew 16:19, "I will give you the keys of the kingdom of heaven; whatever you bind on earth will be bound in heaven.")

Field Notes

CHAPTER EIGHT

A Few Questions About God

This chapter deals with two realms—how to handle doubt and how to cultivate a genuine life with God. Either could fill a book, of course, but this will get you well on your way!

Reflect

> Despite the upbringing I had, or maybe because of it, I feel as though I have wrestled with faith as much as anyone. But I've gotten the impression from a good part of the church that somehow questions are bad, that I just need to "believe." So what do I do with my doubts—just bury them?

. . . If you recall the story of "doubting Thomas," Jesus didn't ignore his questions. Thomas heard rumors of a risen Christ but needed something more to go on than the experience of his friends; Jesus appeared to him personally, and invited him to see for himself the wounds of his hands and feet. He addressed Thomas's doubts directly—no smoke and mirrors; then he urged him to "stop doubting and believe" (John 20:27). Christian faith is not an act of mental suicide. If you feel like something smells like dog squat, you are not expected to go ahead and step in it. (And there is no squat like religious squat.) Many young people feel backed into a corner: turn a blind eye to the stinking parts of religion out of loyalty to their church or a sincere desire to stay with God, or let the squat foul everything and reject faith altogether.

Have you found yourself in that dilemma? What have you done with the doubts you have had?

_____

_____

_____

_____

_____

_____

As a millennial, you have been raised in the culture of postmodernism; no, that's not quite right. You've been gasping for a breath of fresh air in the poison gas of postmodernism. Doubt is now embraced as inevitable, a badge of authenticity. . . .

Doubt has become a sort of refuge—not only from the errors of the past but frankly from the burden of action that clarity requires. Doubt is easy; conviction requires courage. . . . So, to be clear, doubt is not a virtue. Humility is a virtue, including intellectual humility, but doubt in its current cynical form has nothing noble about it when it abandons the search for answers—like a man lost in a city who simply slumps down onto a park bench and stays there.

Did this ring true for you personally, or for friends you have? Why do you (or they) hold on to doubt?

Much of what thoughtful people are rejecting when they reject Christianity is actually the embarrassing parade of Christian *culture*—all the "plastic Jesus" nonsense. It will help you so much to separate Christianity from the carnival of Christian "culture" out there (oh, how I wish the unbeliever could do this, even for a moment!). Big hair, gold thrones, lots of shouting—those are a reflection not on Christianity but on the people who indulge in Vegas-style antics. Music is a great comparison—music in itself is a wonderful gift. But over the years mankind has made some pretty stupid music, some really kitschy music, and some down-right heinous music. That doesn't prove music is stupid, kitschy, or heinous—it only proves people can be. But that's nothing new. The same holds true for sex—people can get pretty bizarre with sex, but that doesn't prove sex is bizarre.

If you could separate Jesus and his teachings from the wacky and harmful Christian cultures out there, how much of your doubts about faith would remain?

Yes, many intellectuals and academics dismiss the Christian faith. But then you have to account for the myriad of equally brilliant men and women who have found in science and history reasons *supporting* their faith. For every Bertrand Russell or Stephen Hawking, you have to account for a Pascal, Dostoevsky, or even Einstein (who believed in God). Your average freshman may not know it, but there is nothing even close to an "intellectual consensus" in rejection of Christianity. Come to think of it, there isn't an intellectual consensus on *anything* in the academy nowadays, so that is hardly a defining statement on your faith.

Were you aware of this—that there are a myriad of brilliant men and women, academics, PhDs, who fully believe the Christian faith? Did you know that there is nothing close to an "intellectual consensus" against Christianity? What does it do for your faith to learn that no such consensus actually exists?

All this to say, your average man on the street has "heard" that the Bible has long been debunked by science or history when in fact nothing of the sort has happened. They've swallowed their culture's assumptions whole without even giving it a day or two of personal investigation.

Have you swallowed your culture's assumptions? What is your position on the Bible—and where did it come from?

There is more support for the Bible than any other ancient manuscript, and more is added every year (the discovery of the Dead Sea Scrolls being one of the highlights of the twentieth century). On the whole we have good reason to be sure the book we read is the book as it was written. As for the reliability of what is contained in those pages, archaeology and historical inquiry continue to confirm claims in the Bible about the location of places and events. David actually was king over Israel from 1010 to 970 BC; Solomon built the temple and we know precisely where; Jesus of Nazareth lived at the time of Herod Antipas. . . .

Really—if the Bible is only the musings of men *claiming* to speak for God, it is just too badly done to pull it off. . . . If the Bible were constructed by men to pose as a divine manuscript, even the sloppiest scribe would have taken out apparent inconsistencies and embarrassing moments. . . . The Bible is too brutally honest to be fake.

What would be the effect if you were fully convinced the Bible was a completely reliable record of the word of God to us?

And what is keeping you from *being* fully convinced?

The Christian faith is at its center an invitation to intimacy with God. He is an actual person, with a personality and a heart just like you, and just as in any other relationship, it is the connection of these two hearts that matters above all else. This is where we separate from religion, and this is what will rescue us from slipping back into it. Friendship with God is the heartbeat of it all; nothing else can substitute (though many things will try).

So, the question is, how do you cultivate friendship and intimacy with God?

How would you answer that question for the earnest seeker, if he or she came to you?

What are your current practices to cultivate genuine friendship with God?

We listed several classic spiritual disciplines as a way of strengthening the warrior in us: silence and solitude; worship and the sacraments; good teaching; the Scriptures. Do any of these play an active role in your weekly life? What might you do to begin to include them?

We also suggested those things particular to your friendship with God—
walking on the beach, reading a great book, listening to music, dinner and
laughter with friends. What do you love to do? And have you connected
God with your love of that?

> The heart is essential for knowing God; the heart is the means.
> Therefore, the more awake and aware, the more healed and available
> your heart is, the more you will find you can connect with God. Pay
> attention to the life of your heart—where are you looking for love,
> or meaning, or comfort, or identity? Take that to God; invite him
> right there. Where are you anxious, or angry, or lonely, or filled with
> joy and playfulness and yearning for adventure? Invite God there.

Do you journal? How do you pay attention to the life of your heart?

> Hang out with people who know and love God—they should be
> the core of your circle of friends. But you can also enjoy their "com-
> pany" through books and by attending their talks. Remember—we
> aren't talking about a nice little addition to our lives; we are in a
> vicious battle for our hearts and everything we love. We cannot
> hope to win without God—*that* is the context for seeking him,
> for cultivating a "spiritual life." This is life and death, not another
> round of "Amazing Grace."

Be absolutely honest—do the people you spend most of your time with contribute to your heart flourishing in a life with God?

Watch or Read

As we said, this chapter deals with two different issues—how to deal with doubt and how to cultivate a genuine life with God. What you need to read or do depends on where you are right now. So we'll address actions for both.

Dealing with Doubts

Read *Orthodoxy* by G. K. Chesterton. Keep in mind that he goes off on tangents and I (Sam) didn't understand everything, but he has some wonderful ways of exploring theology. Or *Mere Christianity* by C. S. Lewis (even the first two chapters will strengthen your faith).And *Atheist Delusions* by David Bentley Hart is a broad historical demonstration about why the New Atheists are wrong and the truth of the gospel is believable. If you like science and philosophy, *A Shot of Faith to the Head* by Mitch Stokes might be up your street.

Cultivating a Life with God

How we perceive Jesus is everything; if we see him as a religious figure, the stained-glass guy, we are going to find it mighty hard to connect with him. So read *Beautiful Outlaw—Experiencing the Playful, Disruptive, Extravagant Personality of Jesus.* You're gonna love it.

Do

Dealing with Doubts

First, dedicate some time for real, honest exploration of what you are struggling with. Take a few hours away, grab a journal, and write down as specifically as you can what your doubts are. It's really healthy to do this and must be intentional if it is to happen. Then take those questions to someone you respect. (That's how this book was born, actually—with Sam bringing to John his questions about how much the Bible is to be trusted.) Seek out a professor or mentor or pseudo-uncle, and ask him some of your questions. Express your doubt if you have it. May it be the beginning of your own book!

But let us raise another really helpful angle here—the enemy is always trying to undermine our faith. As we talked about in the last chapter, this is *war.* Is it possible you have made some agreements with doubt? As in, "I'm just not going to find God," or, "God doesn't speak to me," or, "There really isn't any way to really know if it's all true," or something like that? Break those agreements as a way of fighting for your heart and clearing the air so you *can* get to what is true. We're serious—break every agreement you've made with doubt, out loud, right now. Renounce them. You might be shocked how much of your struggles were actually spiritual warfare.

Cultivating a Life with God

God is a very personal person and he loves to be personal with us. Meaning, there are no formulas to the Christian life. We will recommend some actions here; try a few and see which of these draw you in to a richer experience of God:

Create "relational space" for God. Invite Jesus into one of your favorite ways to spend an hour. Is it running? Riding your bike? Having a good cigar? Do it, but talk to God while you're doing it. Invite him in.

Worship. We mean alone, with the music cranked, or with your headphones on. Just put on some great worship music and spend fifteen minutes there (okay, thirty; it passes so fast). Do this for a week or so and notice the fruit of it. Play worship music in your car too.

Journal. Meaning, not a diary, not a record of the day's events, but a place to write down your internal world, express your heart, and write out your prayers.

Talk About It

If you are doing this with a group of guys, you'll want to split the conversation into two parts—talking about doubts and talking about how to cultivate a life with God.

On doubt—be kind with the doubts that guys express. Don't jump on their case. Offer encouragement, but be gracious.

Talk about the idea that "doubt is not a virtue."

When it comes to cultivating a life with God, talk about what works for you. Where do you find God? What helps you connect with him?

_____

_____

_____

_____

_____

_____

_____

Field Notes

CHAPTER NINE

The Collision of Intimacy

This chapter dives more deeply in to what it looks and feels like to live well toward a woman. Sam is married by this chapter, but we will keep our questions here focused on passages that apply to every man, whatever his situation might be.

Reflect

Susie and I are opposites in so very many ways. We clearly approach sleep differently. She wakes up much like a puppy, all bright eyed and excited to be in a new day, while I am what you might call . . . slow to rise. . . . I run at a steady pace, fit for one that has chosen other things for the past twenty years, that is to say, not always the essence of elegance or speed. Susie runs like the soundtrack to *Chariots of Fire* is audible. . . . She treats every new acquaintance as a best friend, while I have adopted the old judiciary model of "guilty until proven innocent" and wait for the person to win my favor. When Susie is with me, we eat quite well, whereas once

> I am left to my own devices, I dine on Korean Ramen. Ironically, I like nice things and she can live without them quite happily, whereas she pines over good cheese and I am lactose intolerant.

Sam begins the chapter by talking about how opposite he and Susie are. Were you resonating with this? Name some of the ways you are opposite from the woman, or women, in your life.

Have you ever wondered why God made men and women so different? What's your take on that?

> Sartre felt that "hell is other people," but precisely the opposite is true—hell is being left alone forever, with no other reality than your own consciousness of yourself. It is being locked in a casket of your own internal chaos with no hope of a window or door letting in light from outside to give you a moment's respite from yourself. Hell is the refusal of the gift of the Other.
>
> The adolescent views the Other as merely an opportunity to

gain a sense of self: *The Other is here for me.* He is mainly concerned with what the Other thinks of him, how she treats him, and especially how she doesn't treat him. But as we step into a more mature, loving relationship, we realize the Other is here to call us out of ourselves, beyond ourselves.

Our friend Craig calls it "Lovers versus Consumers." Consumers see the Other (the beautiful woman) as a chance to get. The Lover sees her as a chance to give. Where would you fall in the comparison? What do your actions say?

Later in the chapter, while talking about sex, John says that masturbation is the ultimate rejection of the Other: "I don't need you. I don't have to engage you at all." The Lover is all about sacrificing so the Other can flourish, while Consumers just want to get something from it.

Does this put the whole masturbation issue in a new light for you—that it's ultimately about getting arousal while not leading to love anyone or sacrifice for her?

The chapter is talking about men and women in the context of marriage, so maybe it would be good to stop and ask yourself, *What are my feelings toward marriage—and where did those come from?* Are you optimistic? Pessimistic? Fearful? Hopeful? Why?

_____

_____

_____

_____

_____

> Opposites really and truly attract—not only in gender, personality, habits, and lifestyle but also *in our brokenness.*
>
> Domineering men typically marry mousy women; domineering women typically choose milk toast men. Perfectionists often marry someone with massive guilt issues; obsessive-compulsive types marry chaotic spouses. God is in that, by the way—he is using the absolute otherness of your mate to get to the brokenness in you, so that he might heal it. . . .
>
> God is fiercely committed to our transformation; he simply will not allow us to carry on unchanged, and so in his love he gives us . . . our opposite.

Did you know this—that God is deeply committed to your transformation, and that he uses the opposites of men and women to get to that transformation?

_____

_____

_____

_____

_____

How does knowing this shape your views on dating and marriage?

> If I have learned anything in these short months, and it
> is possible that I haven't, I have been made very aware of
> how often I feel like I cannot fill her. Man, was this dis-
> couraging for the two of us. . . .
>
> Susie's relational capacity is beautiful. The trouble
> came when I felt that it was my responsibility to be all
> she needed. This kicked in right after we got married,
> and I think it came from a good place—wanting to provide
> and protect and all that—but the fact is it isn't my role to
> be everything and everyone to her. . . .
>
> On the one hand she felt bad that I couldn't be enough,
> *and* she felt like her need was overwhelming. I felt like
> crap because I couldn't fill her, and I learned that no mat-
> ter how much I tried, I couldn't make a dent, so eventually
> I just stopped trying. Why do something if I can't succeed?
> It's a recipe for feeling like a failure, which I'd like to take
> a pass on, thank you very much.

You guys who have tried to offer and come through for a girl—can you
relate? Sam said the vast need of Susie eventually caused him to want to
pull away. What have you done with the "ache you cannot fill" inside all
Eve's daughters?

> *There's a lot of little girl in there.* Surely you have encountered this. When I say things that sound like her father is speaking to her, it is not going to go well. (Which brings us back to "know her story"!) Are you encountering the woman right now or the little girl?

John named five things all men should know in their early years of marriage; we chose this one to repeat here because it relates to every guy. Did you know this about girls—that there is a lot of little girl inside them? How have you seen it come out? How does it make things messy?

> God gave us sex (which really ought to put to rest once and for all every doubt about his goodness). He is *for* your sexual happiness, so pray for your sex life. Invite the passionate love of God and the wildness of his Spirit into your communion.
>
> Prayer brings me to one last thought—healing past brokenness. More than anything else, this tends to be what introduces trouble into the marriage bed.
>
> *(Readers—You will want to pray through your sexual history—probably first by yourself, though the day may come when you are solid enough in your marriage to pray for each other here. The prayer we've included at the back of the book will prove very helpful in healing sexual history.)*

Guys—this is huge. Whatever your sexual history might be, from mild masturbation issues to multiple sexual partners by the time you reached college, you are going to want to seek your wholeness and restoration here. Pray through that prayer in the back of the book! It will bring such goodness and wholeness. Don't put it off!

Watch or Read

Watch the film *Strictly Ballroom* (a quirky Australian movie that's one of our favorites). Watch how Scott navigates his relationship with Fran— how they both handle family and culture and peer pressure. We love how Fran fights for Scott's heart, and then Scott fights for hers at the end of the movie.

How do Scott and Fran care for each other? Are there things they do that you would emulate or change in your life?

_____

_____

_____

_____

_____

_____

_____

_____

_____

_____

_____

Do

One of the best things you can do for your relationship is to pursue your woman's heart. This can look like a variety of things: booking her a day at the spa if that is something she would enjoy, or maybe going on an adventure together for a day like biking, hiking, or tandem sea kayaking.

Ask her what she would love to do—and then plan a special day doing it! Does she love art museums? Antique stores? The zoo? Do it! (Even though and especially if it isn't really your cup of tea. But don't be a pouter during the day. Enter in and enjoy it for her sake!)

Be the supporter of her inner exploration of her heart. If she isn't aware of her inner world, begin to talk about yours, and invite her into understanding herself more wholly. Get her a book that does the same. Make sure she has time for the girlfriends who draw this out in her as well.

Your drive should be to see more life for her, giving not taking. The best part is that your relationship will thrive because of it.

Talk About It

Start with the Lover versus Consumer idea—going to the woman to get something, or to give something. Talk about how that struck you. Which category do most of the guys you know fall into?

That part about how you just can't fill Eve—where has that proven true for you? And what does it make you want to do?

Talk about what your feelings are toward marriage. Are you optimistic? Pessimistic? Fearful? Hopeful? Why?

What are your dreams for life with a woman? What is the relationship you are hoping for (regardless of whether you are single or married)?

Field Notes

CHAPTER TEN

Racing Toward the Unknown

As we reach the closing chapter of the book, Sam first looks back on some of the "lions" he has faced, and then he looks forward to lions he knows are coming, and he makes the choice to ask God to father him. This is the essence of the journey.

Reflect

Sam names climbing a tall peak, building the Baja bug, going off to college, choosing to become an RA, and pursuing Susie as some of the lions he knows he overcame. This can be such a source of encouragement—you *have* faced lions, but you might not have known it at the time or forgotten it since. Go back and reclaim those!

What are some of the lions you've faced? (You might not even have thought of them as lions, but what fearful challenges have you had to overcome? Auditioning for a play for the first time? Moving to a new school? Giving a speech in class? Trying out for the team? Getting a job? Going on that weeklong backpacking trip?)

RACING TOWARD THE UNKNOWN

As men we always wonder if we are up for the next challenge, the next phase of our lives. "But can I handle *this*?" seems like the haunting question of masculinity, always staring us down. It's not the lions we've killed that capture our attention; it's the ones we know are waiting out there for us in the tall grass. So let me ask—right now, in this moment, at this juncture, where do you feel least sure about yourself?

How about you—where do you feel least sure about yourself? Think back through the categories in this book: dreams, career, money, love, identity, women, decisions, warfare. Where do you feel least developed as a man?

Can you see then that this is probably where God will be taking you in the days and months ahead? What can you do to cooperate, enter in, and embrace the process?

But here's the thing: In some areas I still feel young. I mean, I am twenty-five years old, engaging in many arenas that are for men, but sometimes I still hear the voice of the boy in me.

Yes, I'm surprised how much I still do myself. It's embarrassing how often it happens, really. . . . There are young places within us still, there is a boy within, and it is the boy who often feels overwhelmed by the new mountain in front of us. I still remember how I felt on my wedding day (I was twenty-three just like you) . . . going in for my first "real" job interview . . . promotions . . . the day we said good-bye to family and boarded a plane for Washington DC. . . .

Those feelings can be really confusing. They make us doubt our decisions, feel like we are in way over our heads when in fact it is simply the boy inside freaking out because he feels that he has to handle our lives for us.

Are you aware of the boy inside—places in you that still feel young? How do you typically treat those parts of you?

Every man is part boy and part man. God requires the man to step up and play the man; but to the boy he offers comfort and healing. Be kind to the boy inside. It is the man God is calling to face down the next lion, but the boy he treats with genuine kindness. Do the same—be kind to yourself, your fears, your feelings of inadequacy. Don't despise the fact that places in you still feel young; shame never heals, never encourages, never makes whole. Give grace to those places that feel six or ten or even thirteen.

How can you be more kind to the boy inside, without abandoning your journey to become a man? What might kindness toward yourself look like?

_____

_____

_____

_____

As I look forward into this next season, I am very aware that I have some weighty choices to make. For starters: Will I isolate? . . .

When I lived in California, hanging with guy friends meant drinking together. Almost exclusively. It was fun, and has its place, but if that is all there is to do, it doesn't feel very substantial. Now, when I *did something* with friends, whether it was running or sailing or working on the ranch or writing together, the connection felt much stronger. . . . I know that when I don't have good guys in my life I don't do well.

Sam begins to name some choices he has to make in the days ahead. One of them is choosing to develop strong friendships with guys who help build him up. Do you have guys like this in your life? How much time do you spend together? And if you don't, what can you do to take a step toward developing those friendships?

All play and no work makes Jack . . . seriously undeveloped and useless. The boy suffers action, while the man takes action. When I sold my VW, I needed a bit more money to buy a nicer car, so I sold my motorcycle as well. I knew there wasn't much use for it in Minnesota, but more than that I knew it was a sacrifice that needed making in order to secure a better vehicle for the time being. I did not, however, sell my helmet. I know that motorcycles are in my future. I was not giving up on wildness; I was choosing to play the man and take action.

What "actions" do you need to take to play the man in the days ahead? Get a job? Apply to school? Sell the Xbox? Stop smoking pot? What?

I want a sense of mastery. In reading *Shop Class* I have been struck over and over at the need to feel competent in our world, to be the "master of our own things," as Crawford calls it. Again, the boy gets in here and fakes competency. . . .

Being willing to seek mastery of something, putting in the hours of work dealing with setbacks and the slow learning process, is extremely humbling and empowering. To hold true mastery over anything, be it sailing or building model ships or carpentry or bow hunting or Japanese, it instills the kind of general attitude of competency that sets apart the boy and the man. I can't help but wonder: Will I submit to the process? Will I hang in there?

Where do you want to develop a sense of "mastery"? And what will you do this month to move toward it? Enroll in a class? Join a dojo? Look for a master mechanic to show you how? What?

_____

_____

_____

_____

Crawford has a series of mentors in his journey of motorcycle mechanics, one he calls Fred. Fred is a true master of old bikes, and Crawford takes time to be an apprentice in Fred's shop, learning things that can only be passed down through hands-on training. We all want that, in some capacity, I think. Having a guru or father we can learn from, to guide us down the path of mastery, may be the only way to really know we are heading in the right direction.

Now you are naming a truly deep longing in men. Blaine just commented to me the other day that every young guy he knows wishes that some older man would come along and say, "I've got a revolution; we need you; follow me." So I'd like to suggest that the single most important decision you will make in the coming years, the one that will have by far the biggest long-term impact, is this one: *Will I remain open to fathering? . . .*

There is an independent spirit that comes with the twenties, and in many ways it is right on time. You need to head off into your own life, make your own decisions, and assert your own mastery over your world. But thanks to the divorce generation and the adolescent culture, most young men seize that independent spirit like a banner and never look for any form of fathering. A host of Peter Pans. But as you have discovered, the thrill of self-determination soon gives way to loneliness and disorientation. We were never made to do life without a father; fatherhood is literally at the center of our universe. I know isolation has become our normal and it feels like freedom, but the trade-off just isn't worth it.

Whatever else we've tried to offer in the pages of this book, the backdrop of it all is what it might look like to receive fathering. This is the ache of every man's heart, whether he is conscious of it or not.

Are you aware of that ache? Can you put your own words to it right here and now?

_____

_____

_____

_____

That's not what it feels like at first. What we want right off the bat is a map of some kind, a plan, a clear path to begin walking down. Something that makes it clear what is important for us to do, and how to start doing it right now.

Right, and God doesn't give one. Nobody gets the master plan, not even a five-year overview—have you ever wondered why? The reason is simple and massively disruptive: God wants us to seek him, draw near to him, learn to walk with him, and frankly we won't do it if we have a plan to follow instead. . . .

You have a friend who is trying to figure out if and where to pursue a PhD, a friend who is trying to start a music career, another starting his own business, a fourth who has gotten married but doesn't know what to do next—are any of them asking God to father them? Are they seeking out the counsel of older men? You begin to see what I mean. I love the go-for-it zeal of young manhood, but too often it comes with a generous dose of *I-don't-need-help-with-this* and no fathering ever takes place.

Sound familiar? Does this describe the guys you know? Does it describe you?

It begins with a posture—*I need a father; I have a father; I am going to seek my father.* Isn't that the turning point in the story of the prodigal son? He shook off his independence and took on a new posture, a willingness to turn father-ward . . . and it saved him. . . .

Ask for God to father you, every day. I'm serious. As you wake in the morning, as you drive to work, as you face the new thing, say, "Father, I need you to help me today; I ask you to father me." Begin a practice of asking for it; then remember to ask for it when you realize you haven't asked in some time.

This might be the simplest, most revolutionary step you can take. Will you ask God to father you? Really?

_____

_____

_____

_____

I believe you young men are the warrior generation this world needs. I believe you will see very trying times, perhaps even the end of the age. The timing of *Halo*, the film adaptations of *The Lord of the Rings,* the resurgence of superheroes in film, and all the games and movies like these is curious indeed. Their epic, urgent, heroic battle cry was spoken at this moment in history—your moment. Perhaps it was orchestrated by an unseen hand. You have the strength and the courage to handle what is before you. You do. But you must not try to play Switzerland in this savage war; there is no neutral ground. The only safe move is to boldly take sides with the kingdom of God, take your position in the line. Make the decision to be fully in—to become the warrior, live in the larger story—and everything else will fall into place. "All things shall be added unto you." Really.

Are you ready to be "fully in"? To enter the process of becoming a warrior? Are you at least ready enough to pray this prayer . . .

My true Father in heaven, Father of Jesus Christ—I'm yours. I give myself utterly to you. I choose sonship; I want to be your son. I choose train-ing; I ask you to father me. I renounce my independence; I choose a life with you. I renounce the ways of this messed-up world; I choose the ways of your kingdom. I ask you to come and guide me on my journey. Father me, and provide fathers for me. I pray for validation; I pray for love. I pray you would speak deeply into my identity. Help me to walk away from the false self and from the opinions of others. Help me learn to hear your voice. I pray for competency; I pray for mastery. I choose the process of becoming a man. Guide me as I navigate the world of dreams and career, of money and finances, of women and love and dat-ing and marriage; guide me as I make decisions and face the warfare set against me and others; prepare me for the road that is before me. I give myself to you, to be your son. Father me. I'm in.

Watch or Read

If you want to carry on the journey, we really do urge you to read *Wild at Heart*, and if you have read that, read *Fathered by God*.

Star Trek (2009) is a great story of stepping up into becoming the man you are supposed to be, as well as showing how fathering can come from more than one figure in our lives.

The King's Speech is another interesting depiction of fathering. Watch the relationship develop between King George VI and Lionel Logue, and more importantly how Logue invites the transformation of the king.

Garden State might be a little rougher around the edges for some of you, but the story's merit lies in its focus on leaving behind the boy by dealing with what has been holding back the young man.

Do

Permit us to repeat this one simple action:

> As you wake in the morning, as you drive to work, as you face the new thing, say, "Father, I need you to help me today; I ask you to father me." Begin a practice of asking for it; then remember to ask for it when you realize you haven't asked in some time.

Build friendship with some guys—plan an adventure trip! It doesn't need to be epic. Do a road trip somewhere. Go camping. Catch the Final Four or some big game together. Whatever.

Pick one area you know you need to grow in—handling money, stepping toward a woman, dreaming about a new career, getting in shape—and name a significant action you can take in that direction. Take it.

Talk About It

This book, and the journey that we have been walking along, really ends with the hope of further fathering. It's an invitation to seek out God in a new dimension. How often we call him "Father" but so rarely ask what we would like to ask were he an earthly person. Talk to one another about that invitation.

Is this something that some of you are walking in already, or does it seem like a nice concept that you have a hard time living out?

_____

_____

_____

Sometimes we struggle with leaving the "boy" behind to become the "man," but the healthy route may be to keep the wonder and excitement of the "boy" while living out of the strength and capability of the "man."

Have some of you pushed off stepping up to become the man for fear of losing what boyhood has meant to you? Have others of you killed the places of wonder for the sake of feeling strong? It would be good to talk about what a healthy coming of age should look like.

_____

_____

_____

_____

_____

Be honest with one another about how helpful this book has been for you. Have you dived fully in to the conversation, honestly questioning yourself and your world, or did you hold back? What do you feel going forward?

_____

_____

_____

_____

_____

You guys have taken a journey together in this workbook—time to take an adventure trip together. Make it the big climax of the experience. Plan a trip you can pull off in the next couple of months. You will love it!

Field Notes

What next? Where do I go from here?

It is our hope that after reading the book and completing this journal, each of you will feel more equipped to face the world as a young man. But the journey doesn't end here. We have created an online magazine in the ethos of inviting active community as we continue to explore what genuine masculinity looks like. It's called *And Sons* magazine. Come check us out: www.andsonsmagazine.com.

Those videos we've mentioned from our trip to Moab—we created them for you! They're free, so check them out: www.KillingLions.com.

We are doing live events for men. Come and join us! Check out "events" at www.ransomedheart.com.

Finally, cheers to you for taking the step to journey into this wilderness with us. We doubt it has been an easy road, but the fruits are worth it. Way to go! We're proud of you!

Field Notes

Field Notes

Field Notes

Field Notes

Field Notes

Field Notes

Field Notes

Field Notes

Field Notes

Field Notes

Field Notes

Field Notes

Field Notes

Field Notes

Field Notes